D1509482

MAKING
THE MOST OF
STORAGE

MAKING
THE MOST OF
STORAGE

DEBORA ROBERTSON

RIZZOLI
NEW YORK

For my parents who, eventually, made me tidy

First published in the United States of America in 1996 by
RIZZOLI INTERNATIONAL PUBLICATIONS, INC.
300 Park Avenue South, New York, NY 10010

First published in Great Britain in 1996 by
Conran Octopus Limited
37 Shelton St.
London WC2H 9HN

Text copyright © 1996 Debora Robertson
Design and layout copyright
© 1996 Conran Octopus Limited

All rights reserved
No part of this publication may be reproduced in any manner
whatsoever without permission in writing from
Rizzoli International Publications, Inc.

ISBN 0-8478-1937-X
LC 95-71192

Project Editor   Jane Chapman
Art Editor   Alison Barclay
Picture Research   Claire Taylor
Production   Julia Golding
Illustrator   Sarah John

Printed in Hong Kong

CONTENTS

MASTERPLAN

Most of us have, quite literally, more possessions than we know what to do with. We hoard objects in the hope that they will be useful one day and when that day dawns, we have long since forgotten where we put them.

If every cupboard is bursting at the seams, every surface groans under a mound of paper and a simple DIY job sends you into a frenzy of drawer and door opening, it is time to take a good look at what you've got, how you use it and, above all, how you store it.

ASSESSING YOUR NEEDS

You've found a home you love, you've moved in and you've started to unpack. Suddenly the space that looked so generous begins to show some of its limitations. Or, you moved in ages ago and since then you've added a couple of children, acquired a pet or two and taken up a space-consuming sport or hobby.

In most households space is at a premium, but most of us have much more at our disposal than we think. We all have a drawer stuffed with receipts, lone batteries of undefined efficacy, and menus from restaurants that have long since gone into receivership. We all have a shelf stuffed with fading newspapers and magazines and a cupboard crammed with a spaghetti of shoe laces and broken rackets. Creating the perfect storage system is about banishing this clutter and filling these wasted spaces with the practical, precious or pretty.

The first step on the road to this goal is to look closely at the way you live your life. The storage requirements of

BUILT-IN SOLUTIONS

Using smooth lines and a simple, strong colour scheme can integrate even the most complex storage system into a room in a seemingly effortless way.

Walls and woodwork painted in shiny white gloss keep this beach house shipshape (previous page, left). The simple, uncluttered scheme disguises a number of ingenious built-in ideas including the deep shelf under the window for housing records. Window seats with lift-up lids create a home for bulky items, such as extra folding directors' chairs for guests. Above eye-level, a Delft rack holding a collection of plates adds colour.

Neat bookshelves look smart in this light and airy country home (previous page, right). Cupboards below waist height hide less attractive items and have sliding doors, which are more economical on floor space than hinged ones. To add visual variety, an alcove housing logs complements the relaxed feel of the scheme perfectly.

ACCESS ALL AREAS

When it comes to planning a small space such as a studio apartment, squeezing the most out of every inch is vital if you don't want to end up in unbearable chaos. It is also important that furniture and fittings look good from every angle to contribute to the overall scheme.

In this compact studio (left and far left), clever use of space and luxurious textures combine to create a living area that is both stylish and practical.

Kitchen space is divided from the living area by shelves and cupboards which, helpfully, open on both the cooking and eating sides.

Crockery stacked on deep shelves demonstrates that in a small space your storage system should not only be well organized, but should also add to the aesthetic appearance of the whole room.

COLOURFUL CLASSICS

For many of us, the living room is our most generously proportioned space. But we often walk a tightrope between transforming it into an elegant living area and successfully finding a home for all of our possessions. Frequently, this task is made more difficult because the living room has to double as the location for a plethora of equipment.

It can, however, be a happy marriage if, at the initial planning stage, you take trouble to integrate all of the diverse demands on your space. You can even use your storage requirements to decorative advantage.

In this stylish Dutch apartment, traditional-style shelving units are painted in a striking shade of brick red and lined with boxes covered in a smart check plaid. Infinitely practical, these decorative boxes swallow up a great deal of household clutter and also contribute to the room's visual impact by tying together the warm colours used for the furnishings.

If you want to try this, you could colour code the boxes. For example, use red for sewing equipment, yellow for stationery, and orange for tapes and CDs to create dramatic bands of colour in the room.

a home-centred family of five, for example, will differ markedly from those of a young woman living in a tiny studio, but the basic principles are the same.

Personal best

It is essential to take into account your storage 'type'. If by nature you are a hoarder with a shelf full of old trophies and family snapshots, you may clear out your home to a state of Japanese-like minimalism, but within weeks your possessions will start to encroach on your new, clear space and you'll be back where you started. If you have a penchant for collecting junk and avidly hunt out second-hand shops, you need to take account of this when you begin to sort out your home.

Conversely, if overstuffed shelves tend to drive you to distraction, you need to find ways to hide your possessions. We all have to strike a balance between our desire for order and our storage type to create a realistic solution that will last a lifetime rather than a few, virtuous weeks.

Creating solutions

Every household is an evolving entity. Partners and pets come and go; children grow; our interests change. Throughout our lives, we collect things we are reluctant to jettison when their relevance diminishes.

The first step in creating a working storage system is to examine your possessions and the space in which you keep them as objectively and dispassionately as you possibly can. Try to look at your home as though you are seeing it for the first time. Examine every nook and cranny and assess the storage potential of each one. At this stage, don't think about what you need to buy but what you need to store.

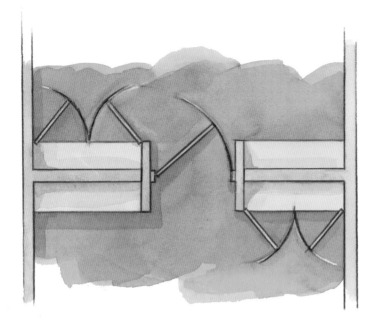

Building a wall of cupboards and shelves (left) is an effective way of dividing a room and, depending on your requirements, it could solve all your storage problems straightaway. Choose between the sleek look of smart cupboards or the dramatic impact of a wall of carefully arranged shelves.

Depending on your floor space, you may also wish to consider sliding, retractable or concertina doors as they don't impinge on the room as much as hinged ones do.

Be as ruthless as you can and give away, swap, sell or throw out all the things you no longer need or want. To inspire you, think how good you will feel when you are no longer tripping over that hall stand with the funny leg or dusting the dinner service you got for a wedding present but have never used. In your new, perfectly ordered state, think very carefully before making any new purchases and only let a sizeable new object into the house after you have discarded an old one. It's a simple trade-off system and it works.

To make the most of your newly available space, it helps to keep the solutions simple. You should be able to locate your golf shoes, your cake tins or the family's passports without having to hunt through drawers, cupboards and boxes. In general, it's a good rule to store objects as close as possible to the place where you use them. Items you use together, such as hammers, drills, nails and other DIY equipment, should all be kept in the same place. By the same token, don't keep your sewing machine in the understairs cupboard, your needlework basket in the sitting room and your scissors in the kitchen.

Making priorities

Consign things to first, second and third priority. As a rule of thumb, the most frequently used items should be allocated to the prime position, between waist- and eye-level; things of secondary importance, or heavy items, should be stored below waist height; and objects you require infrequently can be relegated to above eye-level space. If you apply this rough principle to a study, for example, frequently used items such as word processors, diaries, basic reference books and stationery should occupy the prime position; household accounts and other files could be kept in secondary position; and anything that you use only occasionally can be stored in the less valuable space above eye-level.

CARVING UP SPACE

If you are feeling cheated on space, there is no need to feel cheated on style. In the planning stage, this small studio was divided into practical spaces without sacrificing the room's simple, airy qualities.

When the doors are closed, the room looks as though it is finished with a chic wall of flush cupboards and well-lit display areas. When opened, high cupboards disguise shelves for books, papers and magazines; central doors open onto a well-planned galley kitchen; and the other doors conceal a neat shower room and the entrance to the bedroom.

WALL WORKS

When you have lots of things to store, often the best solution is to have a whole wall of cupboards or shelves.

If you choose cupboards, the type of door you decide on will have a huge impact on the room's overall appearance. Imagine the different impressions created by mirrored doors, door frames filled with shirred fabric or chicken wire, or sliding panels with a high-gloss paint or laminate finish.

In this bedroom (right, above), simple doors are backed with inexpensive reed blinds which harmonize perfectly with the room's natural textures and also allow air to circulate around the clothes.

In some instances a whole wall of shelves works best. This can look particularly effective when the shelves are constructed along a door wall. In this small kitchen (right, below), a run of wall-mounted cupboards could induce claustrophobia, making the room look even smaller than it is. Open shelves keep spices and recipe books close at hand and make the most of the room's modest proportions.

In this dining room (far right), deep shelves store and display glasses, dishes, drinks and decanters in close proximity to the table.

A clean sweep

Don't try to do everything at once. Make a list and break down what you need to do in order of priority. Give yourself a timetable and do a little each week. Obviously this doesn't work if you are planning a massive remodelling job, but for most of us – for whom tidy cupboards, a few more bookshelves and well-organized kitchen cabinets would improve our lives immeasurably – it's a good way of making steady, noticeable progress.

Remember, an effective storage system isn't about an alphabetized CD collection or a sock drawer that goes from pastels to primaries in rainbow-like degrees of gradation, it is about reclaiming precious time throughout the day. Every ten minutes you don't spend frantically hunting down your car keys is ten more minutes you can spend doing something more worthwhile.

FIRST STEPS

Tailor-made storage solutions are the ones that really work. Use this checklist to help you assess your needs.

- Make a list of the things that consistently annoy you. Nowhere to put sports equipment? A jumbled kitchen? Clothes that burst from the wardrobe? Work out your list on a daily, weekly and monthly basis.
- Do you like having things on display, or do you prefer things concealed?
- What is your budget? Traditionally, the best storage has been expensive.
- Do you have outdoor space such as a shed or garage that could be put to more effective use?
- Do you have any indoor spaces such as attics, cellars or understairs cupboards that aren't as accessible or useful as they might be?
- Are there functions you would like to integrate into your home, such as setting up a home office or sewing area? Do you entertain a lot, or would you like to?
- Can other members of the household be more responsible for their possessions? Coat hooks and shoe racks positioned near the door make it less likely that things end up heaped on chairs – or on the floor.

STORAGE SYSTEMS

Once you have decided exactly what it is you have to store, the enjoyable part starts. You can begin to experiment with different styles, finishes, textures and colours until you have a storage system that not only works successfully, but also plays an important part in your decorative scheme.

Choose from freestanding storage such as bookshelves and cupboards, built-in units or modular systems that you can adapt or take with you as your circumstances change.

MAKING CHOICES

After you have quantified and planned your needs, the next step is to decide on a storage system that will meet them. Many factors affect this, but the dominant ones are budget, space, personal taste and how long you intend to stay in a place. As your system evolves, you will probably find that a combination of storage types specifically tailored to the function of each room, and the way you live in it, works best. Built-in furniture, modular units, freestanding pieces and, of course, shelves, will form the staples of your system.

The drawing board

Before you begin on a major overhaul of your home, even if you are going to get professionals in to help you, it is a good idea to arm yourself with an accurate floor plan. Use a metal tape measure rather than a fabric one, as they can stretch with use, and make your drawings to scale on graph paper. Remember to include recesses, alcoves, window bays and any existing built-in furniture you wish to keep. Make a note of the height of windows, fireplaces and architectural mouldings and the way doors are hung.

The next step is to look at your furniture requirements. Measure the pieces you are going to keep and draw them on same-scale graph paper. You could use one colour for existing furniture and another to indicate pieces you want to build or buy. Once you are satisfied that essential freestanding pieces have found their natural place, start to plan built-in cupboards and shelves.

At this stage you may also decide to measure the things you want to store and consider their weight, so that you can devise the strength and size of drawers and shelves. Try to be generous in your estimation of the amount of space needed for the opening of doors and drawers and for people to move comfortably around the room.

Built-in options

Built-in furniture is permanent and can be expensive, so you may wish to consider how long you intend to stay in a place before you make any major commitment of time and money. However, it often represents the most efficient use of space and can be tailor-made to exploit any awkward and unused spaces you may have. An additional advantage is that you can also specify the perfect decorative finish for your scheme.

Take a good look at the room you are working with and note proportions, architectural details, recesses and any usable walls or corners. If you are going to create a whole wall of cupboards, ensure that door furniture and any mouldings, such as beading or cornicing, match those used in the rest of the room. You may even want to re-create a scaled-down version of the existing door panelling for your cupboard doors.

Creating the impression that cupboards are a continuation of the wall can look very elegant. You may also want to try finishing cupboards with paper, paint or even fabric used elsewhere in the room to draw the whole scheme together. You may also wish to incorporate large pieces of furniture, such as a desk, table or sofa, into your storage wall. Creating an alcove with shelves or cupboards will give the room a sense of order and, in a

THE APPROPRIATE SOLUTIONS

The best, most effective, storage systems play an integral role in the room's overall appearance. If you find something unattractive or jarring on the eye, you are less likely to maintain it.

In this well-ordered bedroom (left), simple glass shelves make an elegant and understated display area for this attractive collection of ceramics without detracting from the sculptural quality of the open staircase.

Inexpensive drawer units have been used to create a smart storage unit that ties in perfectly with the modern furniture in this attractive Dutch apartment (page 16). Each unit has been painted in three different colours and stacked with a sheet of thick glass between each layer and on the top to create ample space for books, lamps and photographs. The interchangeable drawers allow different colour schemes to be achieved.

A demonstration that improvised storage ideas are often the best is also provided by this 50s shop dummy (page 17). The addition of some butcher's hooks has transformed it into an original and practical home for these colourful mugs.

DRAWER DEAL

Integrating the technological trappings of modern life into a decorative scheme represents a challenge to even the most ingenious of decorators. Ready-made pieces are often too small for all but the most modest collections, so you are better off either making your own from scratch or adapting other, larger pieces of furniture.

Here, a deep shelf housing audio equipment sits snugly beneath cupboards containing books, records and videos. Below, a clever drawer system holds an extensive collection of records, exhibition catalogues and magazines; double drawers maximize the space available for cassettes and CDs. And all of this is achieved without breaking the cool, sleek lines of this modern apartment.

small room, can give it a strong, intimate look that makes the most of its limited proportions.

When it comes to the inside of cupboards, look at kitchen manufacturers for ideas on how best to exploit the interior space (see Kitchens and Dining Rooms). For example, the semi-circular carousels normally used to store pots and pans can work equally well in a bathroom, study or garage as they allow you complete access to the deepest part of the unit.

Switch onto lighting

This is also a good time to consider different ways of combining lighting with your built-in storage to maximum decorative effect. Lighting fixed to a dimmer switch and concealed behind pediments at the top of shelving units casts a pleasant, diffuse light; small halogen strip lights hidden behind decorative shelf edging look very effective and the trim helps to conceal the brackets, too. Use tiny spot lights to create stunning accent lighting which can elevate even the most modest display into something rather special. Task lighting is also effective in built-in desk and closet spaces.

Modular methods

Modular furniture has evolved to meet the changing needs of modern life. It combines both open and closed units and drawers for storage and decoration; its great advantage is its versatility, as you can add extra units when finances or space permit. You can also take it with you when you leave, so it represents a good investment.

Modular units are available either ready-made or in kit form, depending on your level of DIY skill. Some pieces are

A wall of built-in shelves with generously proportioned dividers can help to frame even the most disparate collection of items – from books to *objets d'art*.

These deep shelves even help to impose an appearance of order on the casually arranged books (right). They also demonstrate how the best storage systems look best when in use, rather than in their brand-new, pristine state.

BEAUTIFULLY BUILT-IN

A built-in cupboard can solve all your storage problems in one stroke and is often the most space-efficient way of banishing clutter. In some situations, however, it could dominate the room and look rather too overwhelming for comfort. To reduce the possibility of this happening, exploit the decorative possibilities open to you.

These floor-to-ceiling cupboards (left), painted in a soft shade of cream, have an interesting panel detail and curve slightly to give them an elegant, unbroken appearance.

freestanding, while others, particularly those that are fitted one on top of another, will require you to fix them to the wall or floor – as well as to each other. With this particular kind of furniture, it is important to store heavy items as low as you can for stability.

You can also use modular furniture to improvise a dividing wall. This can be useful if you wish to carve a separate dining room out of a large living room, for example, or create a homework corner in a child's bedroom without having to call in the builders.

You can add to modular pieces according to your needs and budget and they tend to have a long life span. In first homes and flats they are often used in sitting rooms and main bedrooms as the sole type of storage furniture, but as

a householder's circumstances change, the modular pieces start a new life in children's rooms, spare rooms, utility rooms and garages.

Freestanding flexibility

Most of us use existing pieces of freestanding furniture such as bookcases, cupboards, chests, wardrobes and trunks as the starting point in developing our storage systems. You may wish to invest in this kind of furniture, as you can always take it with you when you move. However, bear in mind that some pieces may become outdated or could be the wrong size for your new house.

It is a good idea to look at freestanding furniture with an open mind: don't be bound by convention. If you think

MODULAR METHODS

Modular shelving units such as these could represent one of the most flexible, inexpensive and portable solutions to your storage problems (right). You can alter the shelf heights to suit your individual needs, add to the units when space and budget allow and take it all with you when you move.

These units look best crammed with your possessions. Rows of books, decorative objects, pretty boxes and drinks trays draw the eye away from the rather basic construction of the shelves.

In an ideal world, we would all like to have cupboards that seem larger on the inside than they look on the outside. Though in most homes this may be an impossible dream, we can make the space we do have work as hard as possible.

Rails should be supported every 75cm (2½ft) and you should allow roughly 125cm (4ft) of hanging space per adult. Dresses and coats need at least 170cm (5½ft) of hanging length; shirts and jackets require 100cm (3¼ft). And remember, if you cram your wardrobe too tightly, you may as well forget about ironing your things before you hang them up.

laterally there is almost no limit to the number of creative adaptations you can come up with. For example, there is no reason why you shouldn't take a cupboard out of the bathroom or bedroom and put it to use in the living room as a drinks cabinet with drawers for cutlery and tablelinen.

Metal filing cabinets can take a whole host of items, not just the usual paperwork. Use them in the kitchen for pots and pans, or in the bedroom to store sweaters. They can often be snapped up second-hand at auctions and look dramatic when painted or stripped to reveal the metal underneath. Try your hand with car paint sprays, which come in a wide range of metallic or non-metallic colours, or try a local garage. Sometimes they will respray objects for you at a modest cost.

Wooden, fabric or painted screens can be a great ally and are especially useful for dividing storage areas from the main room. You can line fabric screens with deep pockets and wooden ones with small, lipped shelves to maximize their usefulness.

Look out for pieces of furniture that have an element of storage designed into them: coffee tables with a shelf underneath for magazines and books; beds with drawers to hold extra bedding. Alternatively, you can buy ready-made drawers on castors that are designed specifically to slide beneath non-divan type beds. Make sure that each piece is working as hard as it possibly can to justify the space it takes up in your home.

Shelving staples

Shelving is perhaps the most important element in any storage system and comes in all shapes, sizes and styles. Whether you favour wood, glass, aluminium or steel, there

ADAPTABLE ANSWERS

By definition, freestanding storage gives you the most flexibility. As you move units around, you can use them to define different areas in the room. In this loft (left), an old bookcase has been customized to create a wall between desk and studio space. A striking diamond pattern disguises the chipboard back and shows how paint, that most versatile of tools, can be a stylistic lifesaver for the thrifty decorator.

SCREEN STEALER

Be unconventional! Televisions and many of the units designed to house them seldom add much to a decorative scheme, so think laterally. An unusual dresser (left) built into the chimney breast of this Adobe-style bedroom hides a wide-screen television and also a VCR – without compromising the overall look of the room. Take your inspiration from this and hunt down cupboards and dressers to adapt in a similar way.

are ready-made shelving systems around that will complement your scheme. You can also experiment with creating simple shelves yourself or have someone custom-build them for you.

The most practical type of shelving you can buy consists of slotted metal uprights with brackets – and it's also one of the simplest to install. If you are planning several shelves, one on top of the other, measure the height of the things you wish to store and space the shelves accordingly. If you have lots of tall books, it looks better and is more economical on space if you store them laid flat, rather than leaving huge gaps between shelves.

In a wall of shelves, the deepest item should determine the width of the shelf. For bulkier items such as a television or a music system, this may be impossible so you could

consider creating a break-front cabinet effect by combining shelves with deep cupboards.

If you don't have room to add cupboard space, it's important to take care with the weight of the things you put on your shelves. Usually, brackets are placed 40cm (16in) apart, but you should bring them closer together for really heavy loads. Televisions and VCRs require heavy-duty support brackets with special fixings to attach them to a solid wall. Hollow plasterboard walls will simply not take the weight.

Decoratively speaking, the choice of different kinds of shelving can be overwhelming. In a traditional-style room, shelves made from inexpensive pine can be finished with beading or pre-cut lengths of decorative trim and then painted to complement the scheme. Remember, the soft

This attractive window seat (above) provides storage space for a set of folding chairs, but it could be used to hide other pieces of furniture such as a single folding bed or a small card table.

You could make a simplified version with a wooden frame disguised by a curtain. A seat with front, rather than top, access is a great place to keep telephone books, videos and magazines. And you don't have to disturb the cushions – or the cat – each time you need to gain access.

sheen of eggshell almost always looks more sophisticated than shiny gloss. In children's rooms, unsealed wood can be treated with a brightly coloured woodstain and then varnished. For kitchens, workrooms and high-tech interiors consider the possibilities of industrial metal shelving.

Glass shelving can be an attractive way to store beautiful objects in an elegant urban scheme, particularly when it is combined with subtle accent lighting. Ask a glazier to cut the glass for you; it should be plate glass that is at least 6mm (¼in) thick and have the edges ground smooth to prevent you from cutting yourself. As an alternative to glass, you could use clear acrylic Plexiglas or Perspex. It is safer and is available in a good selection of

colours. The only disadvantage is that it tends to be rather more expensive and can scratch easily.

To give existing shelves a romantic, country-style facelift fix lace, paper or scalloped fabric trim along the edge with glue, upholstery tacks or double-sided tape. Small shelves can increase the usefulness of cupboards enormously. Plastic-coated wire shelving with a lipped edge was initially designed for use in the kitchen but you could use it in a bathroom cupboard to store medicines and cosmetics, or in the bedroom to hold scarves, belts and other accessories. Alternatively, line the back of full-size doors with small shelves. This works particularly well in a kitchen, where you can use the shelves to store herbs, spices and seasonings.

UNCONVENTIONAL THOUGHTS

In more traditionally decorated rooms, modern storage units simply don't look the part. The solution is to look out for old pieces of furniture that you can adapt. These don't have to be fine pieces, in fact it often works best if they are a little worn and battered. That way, you don't feel constrained from experimenting as you rip out the insides and slap on coats of paint, woodstain or varnish.

This country-style chest of drawers (centre left) harmonizes perfectly with the rest of the room and the middle drawers have ingeniously been removed to create a convenient space for this record collection.

Using the same principle, try to exploit the natural storage opportunities that each room presents. A stone alcove in this understated bedroom (left) has been lined with shelves in order to hold a wide selection of bedtime reading without compromising the room's uncluttered look.

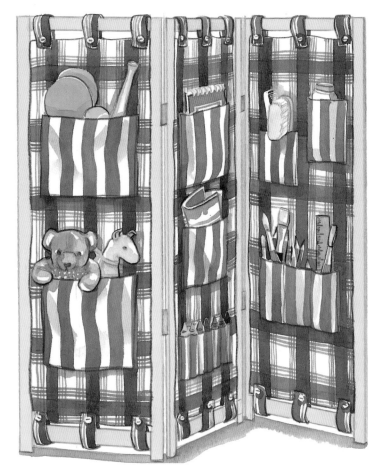

You could find use for a screen in almost any room in the house (left). Screens give you flexibility to divide up rooms into specific areas; use them to disguise a study or hobby corner. Lined with pockets, as here, they keep objects close to hand and free up shelf or floor space. They are available in kit form and can be covered in paint, paper or fabric to suit your individual scheme.

SMALL COMFORT

Really effective storage is about simple ideas that make your daily life easier. And just because something is practical it doesn't mean that you can't inject some fun as you go along. There is a wealth of colourful and clever merchandise on the market designed to do just that – or you could experiment with your own ideas.

Banish tangled socks by lining drawers with small boxes which allow you to see at a glance exactly what you've got (left). Equally, you could use the same system for scarves, underwear or even T-shirts.

Wooden cutlery trays are just one of a number of everyday items that lend themselves to customizing (right). Paint, decoupage, stamping and stencilling are all quick and easy ways to make the transformation.

If you are mad on colour, there's no reason why you shouldn't really go to town. As this kitchen unit (far right) demonstrates, practical doesn't have to mean dowdy. Bright baskets blend with wicker ones and the open shelves are crammed with kitchen staples. The unit is also on castors, so you can keep it close at hand while you're working and then roll it away when you're not.

Improvised inspiration

Instant shelves have graduated from their student days of a dozen or so building bricks and a few planks of wood. Go for glitz and use goldfish bowls full of bright beads to divide elegant bevelled glass shelves. Remind yourself of seaside holidays with old-fashioned metal buckets in bright colours supporting roughened pieces of wood; fill them with pebbles to keep them stable. Pick up architectural mouldings from salvage shops or buy new ones to prop up a quick shelf. Turn a desk into a home office space in minutes by stacking wooden shelves on open-fronted wooden boxes. Use the boxes for pens, stationery, staplers and other necessary items.

Create attractive and inexpensive 'rope ladder' shelves using planks of wood with holes bored in each corner. Thread fine rope or wire through the holes and tie knots to

create the spacing you want, then hang them from the picture rail using special hooks. And for really cheap and instant shelving you could always use building bricks; eminently versatile, you can paint them, gild them or cover them in mosaic or decoupage depending on your decorative scheme – simply use your imagination.

Small wonders

In the midst of all of this planning, it's easy to forget that the things you do to your home should also be fun. Think creatively and look at each storage problem as an opportunity to create a mini still life. Experiment with contrasting colours and textures and don't stop until you're thrilled with what you've produced.

There is no reason why you can't transform even the most mundane household item. Paint wooden crates in bright, contrasting colours and stack them to create an instant, eye-catching set of shelves for the kitchen, living room or bathroom; cover old shirt boxes in fabric to create an elegant home for your stationery; store sponges,

loofahs and other bathtime necessities in velvet bags suspended from a gilded pegboard – or go for a more natural variation on this theme with a distressed paint finish and some wicker baskets.

One attractive and practical idea is to stick a picture of a container's contents on the outside so you can see exactly where everything is at a glance. Experiment with traditional decoupage or bright Polaroids to create the look you want. You could, for example, store seed packets, plant labels and twine in a hat box covered in black-and-white photocopies of old-fashioned motifs of garden tools finished off with an antiqued varnish. Or, cover boxes in bright wrapping paper, one for each member of the family, and stick a photograph of them on the outside. These personalized boxes can then be used to store school reports, medical cards, vaccination certificates, passports and other vital pieces of paperwork.

Shop solutions

If you are short on inspiration, look to the highly competitive world of retail for some great free ideas. Shop designers are skilled at balancing the competing demands of concealed storage, display and practicality. Go to a smart boutique or up-market kitchen store and look at the way they combine open-shelf storage with glass-fronted cabinets, hanging racks with mirrored cupboards. Examine how they maximize the storage potential of simple shelving with boxes, baskets and stacking racks, and how they add hooks and pegboards to almost every available surface. They are the masters of making things look as tempting as possible while cramming as much as they can into what is often a small space.

INSTANT APPEAL

Many of the greatest ideas often cost very little to execute. A Polaroid camera is a very useful tool when it comes to imposing order on your possessions. Keep your shoes in pristine condition and perfect order by storing them in shoeboxes; attach a photograph to the side for instant recognition (left). This idea would work equally well for stationery and craft or sewing equipment.

A selection of brown paper bags suspended from a row of nails tacked into the wall is a simple and affordable idea (right). They provide instant storage for hats, gloves and scarves in this hallway, as well as tying in with the natural decorative scheme.

You could create other variations on this theme. For a more sophisticated version, for example, hang damask bags from brass key hooks along a bedroom or bathroom wall.

DON'T FORGET THE DEAD ZONES

Every home, no matter what its size, has its forgotten spaces which can be cleared up and adapted to release their maximum storage potential.

■ Understairs: throw out the junk and look at the space with new eyes. Could it be used as a study or sewing corner? Could you cram in an extra cloakroom or line it with racks to make a miniature wine cellar?

■ Ceilings: high rooms can take hanging racks or 'laundry maids'. Use them for the *batterie de cuisine* in the kitchen, towels in the bathroom, clothes in the bedroom and toys in children's rooms.

■ Picture rails: Delft racks or deeper shelves add visual interest and exploit what is often unused space.

■ Recessed windows: the wooden panelling can be lined with narrow shelves to great decorative effect. Team them with simple Roman or roller blinds and a pelmet.

■ Doors: the space over a door is often wasted and can look great fitted with shelves of books or ornaments. In a corridor, you may also want to add a cupboard or two for extra blankets and other infrequently used items.

KITCHENS AND DINING ROOMS

Perhaps more than any other room in the house, the kitchen reflects its owner's personality. If you exist on frozen food, or if whipping up a four course meal for ten is more your style, it's going to show in the way your kitchen is organized.

There is a wide variety of styles to choose from. Whether you favour a streamlined fitted look or a mixture of old dressers and pine tables, you will find something to suit you. And the same principles of planning, arrangement and storage apply across the board.

THE BASIC INGREDIENTS

The kitchen makes an extremely complex range of storage demands. You need to make space for everything from cumbersome pots and pans to fragile china, from fragrant and delicate herbs to toxic cleaning products. Before you start, make a list of all of the things you expect from your kitchen. Most of us require space for cooking, eating, laundry and, in some cases, an extension to the nursery. Inventive storage is the key to making your kitchen an appealing place to be in.

Begin the balancing act between display and disguise by taking a good look at your existing kitchen, even if you are planning to rip the whole thing out and start again. Make an accurate plan on graph paper and really look at the space you've got. Which aspects annoy you most? Which seemingly small inadequacies have become constant irritations? Could you move windows, doors, radiators or electrical appliances in order to use your space more successfully?

Next, create your own portfolio of imaginative ideas. Visit several kitchen companies, not only to brief yourself on the wide variety of finishes available, but also to see at first hand some of the many ingenious storage ideas the experts have devised. It's a good idea to do this even if you are going to get a carpenter to help you.

When you are deciding on the location of your storage, you must take into account your work triangle: the area defined by the sink, oven and fridge. Leave the smallest workable space between each element and allow sufficient work surface on each side of the oven and next to each appliance. A long stretch of counter is more useful for

stress-free food preparation than several broken up, small ones. Be ruthless about what you store on the surface – only the things that you are constantly reaching for, such as a utensil jar or knife rack really earn their space there. And a clear surface makes you feel as though you are in control. Alternatively, wall-mount as many things as you possibly can. Blenders and their attachments, draining boards, spice racks and electric can openers are all more efficiently stored on the wall.

Kitchens absorb as much money as you want to lavish on them. There is always a more expensive finish, a newer, state-of-the-art appliance. Whether you love high tech or prefer a more improvised look, there is no reason why your kitchen shouldn't function with equal efficiency.

In this rustic kitchen (previous page, left), units with chicken wire doors, shelves, spice racks, a hanging rail and a dresser are all pulled together with an attractive sea-green paint. Colourful and stylish, it is also practical, with utensils, pans and crockery within easy reach.

In complete contrast, all traces of clutter are completely banished from this tiny kitchen diner (previous page, right). A pristine line of flush cupboards conceals appliances and a neat fold-down table just large enough for two.

A generous island unit creates a dividing wall between the cooking and eating space, enabling the sociable cook to chat and share a drink with guests while preparing the food (left).

There is nothing more satisfying to a keen cook than a neatly displayed row of kitchen paraphernalia (right). Bespoke kitchen companies can transform your dreams into reality or, for a more modest price, you can enlist a local carpenter.

SQUEEZING IT ALL IN

In the kitchen it is vital to banish wasted space. Use even the smallest, forgotten spaces to your advantage.

■ A three-tier cooling rack saves counter space when the kitchen is busy and can also be used in cupboards to store plates.

■ Use the plinth space beneath units as extra drawer space. Some manufacturers even conceal a step ladder behind a kick plate here.

■ The space above wall-mounted cupboards is often wasted. Fit extra cupboards up to ceiling height or add a rack to store bottles.

■ Plastic, wood or wicker drawer organizers can be used in cupboards or on shelves to store napkin rings and boxes of herbs and spices.

■ Create a useful noticeboard by painting a cupboard door with blackboard paint.

■ Butcher's blocks on castors provide an extra work surface.

■ Hang butcher's hooks from wall racks made from wooden garden trellis.

■ Have a chipboard panel cut to cover your table. It shouldn't extend more than 30cm (1ft) over the table's edge for stability, but even this should give you room for four more people.

COUNTRY STYLE

Large kitchens can take freestanding pieces of old-fashioned furniture, either in combination with modern units or as the sole form of storage. Chests of drawers, cupboards, shelves, cabinets, metal boulangerie racks and dressers all make wonderful kitchen storage, particularly if you adapt them to suit your individual needs. Top them with marble, slate, end-grain butcher's block or melamine to make a practical surface to coordinate with the rest of the kitchen.

A huge pine table, an Aga and a marble-topped chest of drawers dominate this farmhouse kitchen. Jars, canisters and a striking collection of Spode are stored on generous shelves, and everyday pots and pans are hung from hooks beneath.

Larger, heavier pans are kept on a space-saving pot stand, while less aesthetically pleasing items such as mops and the ironing board are relegated to the tall cupboard by the stove.

The modern rise-and-fall lighting fits in well with the traditional scheme and is extremely practical, casting light exactly where it is needed for food preparation – over the table.

Elsewhere, follow the principle of storing things close to where you are going to use them. Keep your glasses near to the sink or dishwasher and frequently used pots and pans between the oven and sink. Store cutlery and linen close to the table and sink but not inside the work triangle. This means that another member of the household can lay the table without getting in the way of the cook.

Choosing appliances

When you are working out your storage areas, plan for the kitchen you hope to have in the future, not the one you are stuck with right now. You may not be able to afford a dishwasher or a tumble drier at the moment, but work out where you would put them ideally and hide that space with shelves, cupboard doors or a small curtain. When your budget permits, you won't have to squeeze the new appliance into an unsuitable corner just because you didn't invest in a little forward planning. Look out for appliances that either provide you with some storage or are as small as

The antithesis of the English country kitchen in everything but scale, these restaurant-style kitchens (above and right) follow the same principle of storing things close to where they are used. Wire mesh shelves provide generous storage and hanging racks positioned above the stove keep pans within reach. In some kitchens this look can often be rather cold and clinical, and the addition of baskets, jars and a run of tiles can help to add texture and colour.

HIDE AND SEE

A kitchen crammed with interesting
utensils, pretty china and jars of herbs
can be very appealing, especially for
busy cooks who need to have dishes
and ingredients conveniently at hand.

Be warned, however. If you use your
kitchen mainly for reheating pizza, then
your lovingly collected objects can end

up looking like a tired, dusty still life.
Here, preserve jars store and display
colourful resin-handled cutlery (above),
and glass shelves hold tableware and
help to enhance its decorative impact
(right). Glass-fronted cabinets can also
look attractive, but remember, there's
a lot to be said for being able to close
the door on chaos.

possible to fulfil your needs, thus freeing up space elsewhere. For example, choose ovens that come with drawers in the base, fridges with flexible shelving and drawer space, and slim-line dishwashers – these can be up to 20cm (8in) narrower than standard models. Freezers are often full of forgotten food. Upright models are usually easiest to keep track of, but chest freezers can be a lifesaver if you have a large family.

Cupboards, counters and shelves

Relegate infrequently used items to less accessible, high-up spaces – or even store them in another room altogether. The chances are that you use your asparagus steamer or Christmas turkey platter rarely enough for them to be kept in a hall cupboard if space in the kitchen is limited.

Frequently used items should be housed between hip and shoulder height to reduce stretching and bending. Similarly, position wall-mounted cupboards 45cm (18in) above base units so that they are easy to reach but still allow space for small appliances below. Heavy things you use all the time should be within easy reach.

Cupboards often seem spacious but are frequently underused, or piled precariously with stacks of crockery or cans. Where possible, avoid stacking things two deep or one on top of another. Instead, consider adapting the inside of cupboards with several narrow shelves rather than a couple of deep ones. You may also wish to put shelves on runners to create the kind of pull-out trays you find in department store display cabinets, as this allows you access all the way to the back of the cupboard. Use the height, rather than the depth, of the cupboard where possible and add wire stacking platforms for plates or cans.

COVER UPS

The key to effective storage is flexibility. This is particularly vital in the kitchen where our storage requirements are often the most at odds with our available space. Here, two very different approaches have been used to create flexible, functional storage areas.

A glazed wall lined with stainless steel shelves creates practical and accessible cupboard space without cutting out much light. Sleek Venetian blinds add to the smart urban look and allow the chef to hide less attractive items (left, above).

Though different in style, the solution arrived at in this farmhouse kitchen (left, below) is similar in principle. The island that divides the cooking from the dining area has been lined with shelves which are hidden with simple gathered drapes hung from a pine curtain pole. Where possible, it is a good idea to fit cupboards and cabinets with adjustable shelving so that you can alter their layout as your requirements change.

FANTASTICALLY
FLEXIBLE

Some of the best storage ideas can be inexpensive, flexible and fun. This rustic French kitchen (right) is given character with beaten-up paintwork on the chest of drawers, and a touch of whimsy is provided by the freehand painting on the rough wooden shelves.

A similarly improvised air pervades this London kitchen (centre right), with shelves constructed from wooden wine cases housing oils, vinegars and cookery books. When the mood strikes, they are also easily rearranged.

Adding open storage spaces in small kitchens can be a practical solution and can help to avoid the feeling of claustrophobia you can sometimes get with wall-to-wall cupboards.

Avoid shelves that are more than 30cm (12in) deep to prevent banging your head as you work and edge them with a lip or beading to create a more professional, architectural finish. An edging can also conceal strip lighting to illuminate the work surface.

A shelf positioned just below eye-level, approximately 160cm (5ft 3in) from the floor, is useful for storing herbs, coffee, tea and other frequently used items.

Under-counter cupboard or drawer units can be rendered more useful if they are on castors. Though it may look as though you have a run of built-in cabinets, this gives you the flexibility of being able to pull out one section to create an extra work or storage surface. In addition, drawers made from wicker or wire, which allow the air to circulate freely, make this kind of unit the perfect place to store fruit and vegetables.

Adding wire, wicker or plastic baskets on top-fixed runners doubles the storage potential of deep cupboard shelves, as does lining the insides of doors with narrow shelves for spices and herbs. Use hanging racks for stemmed glasses and cup hooks to hang spoons, spatulas and other utensils. Inserting vertical dividers in cupboards or deep drawers creates valuable filing space for chopping boards, trays or baking sheets.

If you have a small kitchen, fitted units will probably make best use of the available space, but there is no reason for these to look bland. You can combine units with shelves and glass-fronted cabinets to display your most dramatic items. If your kitchen really is tiny, think of using wall units on the floor, as they will save you a precious 100mm (4in) in depth and will give you a greater impression of space. It is also a good idea to avoid swing-out doors; go instead for sliding or retractable ones which are less likely to encroach on your floor space. Finally, always try to invest in the best quality fittings you can afford: the smaller the kitchen, the greater the wear on hinges, handles and surfaces.

STEELWORKS

Flexible solutions are not only restricted to old-fashioned or bohemian kitchens. In this modern kitchen, good design makes up for limited space. A stainless steel counter top with mesh shelves creates a generous preparation and storage area, enhanced by drawers on castors to allow them to be pulled out to give extra work surfaces while you cook. A metal pole above the stove keeps utensils close to the preparation area.

Unless you like the 'laboratory' look of some modern kitchens, you probably want to intersperse your counter space and runs of cabinets with personal objects. After all, we spend so much time in the kitchen it is important that it should appeal to the senses as well as being practical. It's a great opportunity to exploit the decorative potential of ordinary objects: a shelf of homemade preserves, bottles of vinegar or a collection of baskets can all help to make the kitchen a more comfortable and inviting place to be.

When you create your display, however, bear in mind that it's best to use the things you're constantly reaching for. Anything that stays in the same place for too long will be prey to the dust and grease that can accumulate.

LIVING ROOMS

A well-planned living room integrates storage into the decorative scheme, using it to enhance the room's sense of order and calm. For this reason, it is vital to consider your requirements before you even begin to pick out paint colours or fabric swatches.

Many of us make complex demands on our main living space, expecting it to double as a home office, children's play area or even a spare bedroom. Use your imagination and exploit your room's natural storage potential.

The storage system you devise should be
appropriate to the style of your living
room, whether that is high-tech chic or
a more improvised look.

This bohemian living room (previous
page, left) uses a combination of
shelves, cabinets and a trunk that
doubles as a coffee table to provide
ample storage without compromising
the room's relaxed appearance.

Ingenuity and an eye for pattern make
a striking impact in this stylish living
room (previous page, right). An old filing
cabinet has been given a coat of paint
and decorated with graphic decoupage
heads; fabric-covered boxes replace
drawers and provide ample storage for
home-office equipment.

Recessed shelves are a practical way
of storing books, records, videos and a
host of other items. These black ash
shelves are on adjustable brackets and
add dramatic impact in this pared-down
living room (right). Elegant built-in
shelves with concealed lighting add
texture, colour and variety to a
restrained scheme (far right).

A PLACE FOR EVERYTHING

A living room functions as both a public and a private space. It is the room in which you entertain guests and it is the place where you relax and unwind after a busy day. In order to fulfil both of these functions successfully, careful planning is essential. Unlike the kitchen, where planning is visibly apparent, in the living room it should be inconspicuous. You don't want it to look too regimented, as the overall effect will be sterile. The best living rooms look as though they have evolved.

Although the importance of aesthetics should never be underestimated, you also need to be practical. You shouldn't have to move a trunk to get to the stereo or clamber over a chair to put the photograph album away.

Adopt the approach that the more you have to do to put something away the less likely it is that you will put it away. Simple storage systems reduce the chances of the room degenerating into a mess and this is especially important in households with more than one member.

When you begin to plan, consider the structure of the room. The position of doors, windows and radiators can be considerable constraints. If they limit your options, is it possible or practical to block them off or move them?

Exploit your natural advantages. Alcoves on either side of a fireplace look good lined with shelves or with a combination of small cupboards and shelves. If you have a non-functioning fireplace, think about filling the space with shelves, drawers or cupboards. Remember, however, that the eye is naturally drawn to this space so make it as visually pleasing as possible.

Make the most of windows and bays by lining them with window seats. Giving them front-opening doors rather than flip-up lids means that you can gain access to the inside without disturbing seat cushions. Awkward corners between windows and walls can be filled with shelves or slim cupboards provided that the curtain treatment is simple – the combination of blinds and a pelmet looks good. In some living rooms, you can also make the most of the space under the eaves or stairs by lining it with cupboards or shelves .

The extent to which you exploit the potential of these spaces depends on how long you plan to stay in the property. If you are renting, or if you intend to move on quickly and think that the cost of building in storage will

HIGH IDEAS

The first principle of great storage is to take account of the architectural demands of your space and turn them to your advantage.

In this bright study, access to high shelves is provided by a library ladder attached to runners to keep it stable. The capacious built-in drawers below have been chosen to harmonize with the room's overall scheme and the wicker baskets make an attractive and easily accessible home for files. A reading corner by the window makes the most of natural light.

On the table, a neat pile of books adds visual interest. You should take into account your storage type before you go down this route, however. Do not confuse stacks with storage: use them primarily for display purposes as any predilection for mess will reduce your living room to chaos in no time.

NATURAL CHARACTERISTICS

Storage should be treated as a positive element in a room's design, with as much imagination put into its appearance as is lavished on choosing a decorative scheme. Remember that using colours and designs that blend in with the rest of the room creates a greater sense of harmony in a small space.

Parquet flooring and a hessian throw combine harmoniously with the tongue-and-groove walls lined with substantial bookshelves (right). Carefully arranged piles of books on the table look inviting and add to the overall atmosphere of the room.

Despite its rather unconventional appearance, this Ron Arad bookcase (far right) fulfils its function perfectly. No one ever said storage had to be dull.

not increase the sale price of your home, freestanding or modular furniture is the most practical solution. There is such a variety of systems available, you are sure to find something to suit your budget and storage needs.

Even very simple shelving systems can provide some wonderful opportunities for display, often helping to draw the eye away from the piece's simple construction. Remember that you can also improve a basic unit's appearance with beading, trim or a coat of paint. To make instant drawer space for less aesthetically pleasing items, line shelves with baskets or boxes covered in paper or fabric to coordinate with your scheme.

Modern storage systems give shelves as much flexibility as possible by making them adjustable to allow for objects in a variety of shapes and sizes. If you prefer to use older, freestanding armoires and dressers, you can always maximize their storage potential by fitting the interior with a simple metal track-and-bracket shelving system.

Dividing rule

In large living rooms, or ones that are required to double as home offices, dining rooms or bedrooms, dividing up the space with some kind of physical barrier is often the best solution. Screens are an obvious choice, but you can also

Storage is as varied as the people who use it. There is no reason why a practical, functional system shouldn't also be softly feminine if that is your preferred style.

This elegant drawing room (left, above) integrates storage into its overall appearance without compromising its light, airy appearance. Window seats make the most of generous, panelled windows as well as concealing substantial storage areas beneath their seats. On the bookcase, fabric-covered files and boxes in pastel colours store household papers and stationery.

In this calm and sunny sitting room (left, below) which also doubles up as a dining area, storage and display are combined in a striking pine dresser. The large glass-fronted doors enable the attractive tableware to be kept on display while at the time keeping it safe and free from dust. The simple china knobs marry perfectly with the collection of cream china and silverware.

use shelves. Wide ones allow you storage space on both sides; narrow ones can be blocked off on one side with chipboard which is then papered, painted or panelled.

Furnishing options

If you look around, you can often find basic pieces of furniture that provide good storage space. Choose side tables with a couple of small drawers beneath the surface and coffee tables with a shelf for books or magazines. Place trunks, baskets or small chests of drawers next to chairs or sofas instead of coffee tables. This is useful if you have a sofa bed in your living room, as an average-size trunk will hold bedding and a small chest of drawers will give your guests somewhere to put their things.

GO FOR COLOUR

Make the most of interesting objects with eye-popping colour. Here, a beautiful set of shelves provides the perfect home for a selection of books and unusual ceramics, but a more modest collection could look equally striking given similar treatment.

Paint the backboard of a simple dresser or set of bookshelves with a selection of bright colours and it will totally transform any display of household objects.

GO FOR DISPLAY

Storage should be visually appealing as well as practical. In the living room, it should also give some clues to your personality and predilections.

- If you are grouping objects together, look at them as if they are a still life and strive for a balanced combination of colour, texture and form. Peruse art books or magazines for inspiration.
- Regular forms are calming to the eye. A shelf lined with identical wicker or wire baskets, depending on your style, is a good way to store toys, trinkets and hobby equipment.
- In high rooms, a shelf at picture-rail level draws the eye upwards, providing a perfect opportunity to show off a favourite collection of china or some stunning prints.
- Small wooden cubes, stained or painted in primary or pastel colours and then arranged horizontally and vertically can make an impromptu desk. You can also use them to store stationery, pens and books.
- Resist the temptation to break up a wall of stereo or television equipment with some cut flowers or pot plants. Even the smallest amount of dripping water from above could cause a serious accident.

Multi-functional society

Most living rooms are required to absorb an enormous amount of paraphernalia such as books and magazines, televisions and videos, music equipment and children's toys. The key is to plan enough storage for the things you expect to acquire in the future, not simply for what you've got right now. Previously pristine surfaces become swamped with papers; once-adequate cupboards burst open to reveal their contents; and shelves groan and sag under the weight of your book collection. The important thing is to think ahead and allow enough space for your possessions to grow.

The biggest headache for many home decorators is integrating electrical and electronic equipment into the living room. Televisions, video recorders and hi-fi equipment all represent their own challenges and come with attendant small items such as CDs, records and videos. If you are not careful they can, at best, end up looking like a horrible mess of trailing wires and, at worst, be potentially dangerous.

Always measure your equipment and check wiring requirements before you build shelving. Remember to allow space to lift lids and load CDs or records. You can now buy neat plastic tubes into which you can feed cables to avoid the 'scrambled' look. Avoid putting speakers on the floor as they take up precious space and run the risk of being damaged. It is a better idea to attach them to the wall with heavy-duty brackets or disguise them among your reading matter on bookshelves.

Having somewhere to prepare drinks can often represent another challenge. Many purpose-built cabinets are simply too small for even the most modest selection

BUDGET BUYS

Bold execution can disguise the simplest of ideas. In this living room (left and far left), some of the least expensive forms of storage are given a style injection with a striking use of colour. A formal combination of yellow and black distracts the eye from a mantel constructed from simple wrought-iron brackets and a piece of pine painted matt black; basic bracket shelving is given a facelift with decorative trim. Books provide their own decorative impact when neatly arranged in rows, while fireplace space is used for art books that are too large and heavy for the shelves.

ALL SHIPSHAPE

In this modestly sized living room (right), a whole wall has been given over to a near-perfect storage system. Shelves store music equipment, books and videos, the TV pulls out from the wall on an extending bracket and a neat desk with elegant glass display shelves breaks up the line.

The whole wall can be closed off with retractable green glass doors which, ingeniously, still allow the television and CD player remote controls to operate.

You can choose to conceal your storage or use it as an integral part of your room's decorative scheme. In this studio (centre right), a wall of shelves divides up the living space and a section of shelf on a pivot changes the angle of the television without altering the line.

and too short for taller bottles or decanters. It is often a better idea to adapt the shelves or cupboards you already have. Place glasses singly on narrow shelves or in specially designed racks to prevent scratches. Bottles of wine are often better stored in the living room, away from the heat and the humidity of the kitchen. Store them on their side in a wine rack, but keep other bottles upright.

Even if you have a young family, there is no need to resign yourself to a perpetually untidy living room. Keep as much as possible off the floor and keep precious things well out of reach. For safety, you may also wish to put child locks on cupboards containing expensive music equipment or alcohol. Provide yourself with a system of quick tidy-ups: trunks, screens, baskets and skirted tables that are large enough to conceal plastic crates are your best allies here.

Think small

If you have a small living room, it is probably a good idea to think of built-in units. They take up relatively little floor space and will swallow up your possessions while still allowing you space for a bureau and shelves for display. Whether you choose to have units made specifically to your requirements or to buy them ready-made or in flat-pack form, there is a wide selection of depths, widths and finishes available.

A solid wall of units can sometimes look overbearing, so try to include some open shelves and glass-fronted cabinets, possibly with sliding or retractable doors. You may also wish to use a combination of full-height and wall-mounted units to create an alcove. Tucking a desk or a sofa into this space can look very smart and create architectural interest in a small room.

When not in use, television and music equipment can be shut away in a cupboard (above), where it is easily accessible but does not detract from the room's formal restraint. The doors will also offer protection from dust and direct sunlight.

Videos, CDs and records need to be stored so that you can see the spines. Arrange records vertically on shelves divided by uprights; this stops them warping and allows you to pull out a small selection without the whole lot collapsing. CDs, cassettes and videos can be stored upright in a cupboard or drawer.

BEDROOMS AND BATHROOMS

Storage requirements in bedrooms and bathrooms tend to be varied and complex. Even if you are lucky enough to have large rooms, striking the right balance between display and order can be a challenge.

They are private, reflective places where we go to recharge, refresh and relax and therefore the kind of clutter you may find tolerable in other rooms is intolerable here. Clever, inventive storage can transform a hitherto unwelcoming spot into a haven.

AND SO TO BED

It is with a heavy heart that many of us consider bedroom storage, as it makes so many demands on our ingenuity. How do we reconcile practical restrictions and requirements with our decorative needs? How do we choose between freestanding furniture, a sleek fitted look or a combination of both? How do we create practical storage for clothes, bedding and sports equipment and still leave space for the antique prints, pretty perfume bottles or leather-bound books that give the room its character?

Liberate forgotten spaces by eliminating the clutter. Do suitcases and sports equipment really need to be kept in the bedroom, or would they be better stored in a deep hall cupboard? Consider all of the options open to you.

Bed solutions

Most bedrooms are dominated by the bed and, with careful selection, this essential piece of furniture can make a significant contribution to your available storage space. Many beds conceal spacious built-in drawers in their base; if yours stands on legs, make the most of slide-out drawers, crates and boxes specifically designed for this area.

As beds require more width than height, you might want to create a bed platform. This leaves room below for cupboards and drawer space. Alternatively, create an open space beneath large enough for a desk or sofa.

Freestanding or fitted?

The type of storage you choose depends on the style of your bedroom and what you wish to store there. Few things look more appealing than a combination of old

wooden armoires, chests of drawers and blanket boxes. If real antiques are a little out of your price range, scour junk shops and local auctions for more modest treasures. These also allow you more flexibility as you are less likely to feel constrained in the way that you adapt them to your own use. For more contemporary schemes, look out for old metal filing cabinets and ventilated gym lockers to store clothes. Use them as they are or paint them with car spray.

Despite the appeal of old pieces, however, it is often difficult for them to meet modern storage demands

A calm, meditative atmosphere has been created in this rustic bedroom (previous page, left). Originally used as a dovecote, the rough walls have been given a coat of whitewash and simple white linen adorns the bed. In such a scheme, it would be inappropriate to clutter the floor with anything but the most essential furniture, so the perches have been used as unusual but attractive bookshelves.

The tall, freestanding cabinet meets practically all the storage needs of this uncluttered bathroom (previous page, right). Its practical combination of shelves and drawers enables everything to be stored in one place and also helps to keep the attractive tiled floor free from clutter.

Above the bath, a metal rail with butcher's hooks attached – an idea more commonly employed in the kitchen – provides a decorative and easily accessible home for a wide range of bathroom paraphernalia.

LONG DIVISION

Many of us need our bedrooms to do
double duty as home offices, hobby
corners or even mini-gyms. To facilitate
this, you may want to construct a
storage wall that divides one part of
the room from another. This can work
well if you have wardrobes and drawers
on one side and use the opposite side
for shelves, small cupboards, hooks or
even a simple built-in desk.

This seaside house makes the most of
appropriately simple shapes and textures
(left and far left). A wall of wooden,
whitewashed shelves and cupboards
harmonizes perfectly with the rest of
the room and serves to divide the
bedroom from the bathroom, providing
storage on one side, display on the
other. The bed sits comfortably in front
of its rustic headboard.

■ 57

DIVIDING RULE

Screens can be the decorator's best friend, particularly if you are trying to fit more than one function into a single space. Whether they are built-in or portable, they are a relatively inexpensive way of combining storage with display. Some manufacturers sell them by the panel, enabling you to finish them off in your own choice of fabric, paper or paint effect.

A built-in screen divides up this attractive bedroom (right) and provides ample storage space for clothes. It is painted a restful green to match the paintwork around the doors and ceiling and its subdued mouldings contribute to the room's architectural interest.

A more impromptu display is created by a four-panel screen in this colourful bedroom (far right). It conceals a storage corner and allows space for a colourful display of favourite postcards.

adequately. They were created in an age when most people had fewer possessions, so it may be necessary to combine freestanding pieces with fitted furniture.

In smaller rooms, although a run of built-in wardrobes reduces floor space, it certainly represents the most efficient use of the room you have at your disposal.

Whether you choose home-assembly units or custom-made furniture, it is a good idea to consider your options very carefully before you take the plunge. Look at several different furniture ranges and make a note of any useful ideas, such as clever shoe stacks, carousels for ties and interior lighting systems, that you may be able to adapt yourself. Once you have made your final plans mark the dimensions of the units on the floor and wall with chalk to give you an impression of the space the units will take up.

If you don't plan to stay in your home for long enough to justify the expense of fitted units or if you're working to a strict budget, there are plenty of ways you can create short-term, inexpensive solutions. Outlets specializing in shop fittings are a good place to find freestanding clothes rails, stacking drawers on castors and metal grids suitable for hanging scarves, jewellery, belts and bags.

DIY warehouses and chain stores stock a wide range of budget furniture you can finish yourself. Very basic pieces can be given a whole new lease of life with the addition of suitable mouldings; a paint effect and even paper or fabric can look good coated with a polyurethane varnish.

Order in the closet

Whether you choose built-in or freestanding wardrobes, the basic principles are the same. As always, it is best to begin from the inside out. Start by working out exactly

what you need to store. Presumably, you only keep clothes that fit, suitcases that still close and exercise equipment that has seen the light of day in the past six months.

Go through your clothes and group them by size: short hanging clothes such as jackets, shirts and blouses; long hanging clothes such as dresses and overcoats. Save time and stress by grouping them by colour, too. Avoid the temptation of skimping on coat hangers: buy the best you can afford, preferably made from wood, and avoid wire hangers as they can spoil your clothes.

Each hanger needs at least 3cm (1¼in) of rail. The rail should also have at least 30cm (12in) of space between it and the cupboard door and wall to allow enough space for the coat hangers. Remember to allow extra space for out-of-season clothes to be hung in plastic or canvas garment protector bags.

Next, make a list of all of the things you need to store folded. This will include anything made from a wool or cotton knit and some linen. Each item needs between 30–35cm (12–14in) of running shelf space and restrict each stack to fewer than five items. Drawers work most efficiently when you can see in an instant what you're looking for. That way you avoid the pitfall of tangled socks and underwear, and T-shirts that are creased before you've even worn them. Where possible, roll rather than stack and look out for specially designed drawer organizers.

Finally, take time to arrange your accessories. Shoes you wear only occasionally can be stored in their boxes. Everyday shoes should be kept on racks or in hanging shoe organizers. Look out for special hangers for scarves, ties and belts so you can see at a glance what you've got. Cup hooks also work well for small belts and bags.

OPEN AND SHUT

A row of built-in cupboards can often look rather overbearing and monotonous, especially in small bedrooms, and many people steer away from built-in furniture for this reason. You can easily counteract this effect, however, by combining different materials or paint effects.

A classic, but simple variation on this theme is used in this well-ordered bedroom (left), where shirred fabric replaces wooden panels in the wardrobe.

If your clothes are simply too stunning to be shut away, consider shop solutions. The kind of handsome, wooden display cabinets formerly found in smart gentlemen's outfitters or department stores can occasionally be picked up at auctions or in antique shops.

Here, handkerchiefs, cravats and cuff links are kept in perfect order in the shop cabinet, and the door of an old antique wardrobe hangs open to display a dazzling selection of ties, shirts and waistcoats (right).

New hanging rails and adjustable shelves can give a whole new lease of life to the interior of an old wardrobe, as can a quick external facelift. Consider painting, liming, stippling or dragging to give a modern and individual look to an old piece.

A wall of shelves in the bedroom can sometimes look rather oppressive, so in some situations it's a good idea to break it up with a combination of colours, textures and finishes.

A simple hanging pole and basic shelves along a wall have been given the five-star treatment to create this stylish and practical wardrobe (above). A decorative MDF (medium density fibreboard) frame helps to soften the line and inexpensive reed blinds conceal the interior.

REFLECTIVE THOUGHTS

Wave goodbye to gloomy, spartan
bathrooms – even the smallest space
should be a luxurious retreat. And
because this is essentially a private
room, you can afford to be a little more
experimental in your approach.

In this stylish bathroom a wall of
glass bricks makes the most of a small
room with no external light and provides
a backdrop for a set of elegant glass
shelves (right). They demonstrate a lively
combination of storage and display with
towels and a colourful collection of
glassware looking equally at home. A
sculptural glass and metal table holds
other bathroom essentials and adds to
the decorative scheme.

This sophisticated bathroom (far
right) shows how the best storage plays
an integral role in the room's harmony.
Tiles, brushed metal and gleaming
wooden floors are reflected in and
enhanced by a stretch of mirrored
wardrobe doors.

BATHTIME BASICS

Bathrooms often stretch our decorative imaginations to the limit. In many modern homes, they are designed almost as an afterthought, carved out of the most unlikely spaces with little or no external light. Cramped and dark, they often bear little resemblance to the luxurious havens we would like to have for bathing and relaxation.

Bathrooms present their own storage problems. Because many have very limited space, anything out of place is instantly noticeable. While displays of pretty bottles and baskets enhance the room's appearance and help make it a more comfortable place to be, you also need somewhere more discreet to store cleaning materials and medicines. If you like the smart look of a fitted bathroom, it's a good idea to scour kitchen as well as bathroom showrooms to get an idea of the wide selection of door styles, handles and finishes available.

If your bathroom is too small for fitted units, consider a combination of open and closed storage. Boxing in the sink to create a cupboard doesn't take up too much floor space but can create enough room for basic cleaning materials, while a mirrored cabinet above the sink will give you somewhere safe to keep medicines.

In larger bathrooms, you have the choice of combining fixed storage with freestanding furniture. Look out for old chests, cupboards or dressing tables.

Shelves can also solve many of your storage problems. Wider shelves will hold towels while narrow ones can add to the overall look of your bathroom if you arrange your prettiest jars and bottles along them. In small bathrooms, it is worth thinking about fitting glass shelves as they will stop the room from feeling too cramped.

WHERE IT MATTERS

If you make it as easy to put discarded clothes into the laundry basket as it is to drop them onto the floor, it is more likely that they'll find their proper home first time around.

Many laundry bags and baskets are simply too small to be practical and can

be aesthetically unappealing, especially in a small space. Turning over a whole cupboard to laundry, therefore, is often a practical solution for busy households. Here, the cupboard under the sink has been adapted specifically for this purpose and a transparent panel provides a quick reminder that it's time to do the washing (above).

BATH CUBES

Because it is essentially a private space, you can give your imagination a free rein in the bathroom. Experiment with styles, themes and colours, perhaps taking as your starting point a few favourite possessions. In this colourful bathroom (right), a nautical theme has been exploited to great advantage. Walls covered in tongue-and-groove timber are lined with cubbyhole shelves crammed with bathtime essentials and seafaring accessories. Roman blinds in nautical stripes conceal less attractive items, and a hanging rack makes the most of the ceiling space and allows room for airing towels and laundry.

A small bathroom requires a degree of inventiveness to prevent it from looking cluttered. The curved doors in this small *en suite* bathroom (left) are complemented by a cabinet housing a neat basin and, most strikingly of all, the depth of the doors allows space for generous shelves for toiletries and books.

BATHROOM BLISS

Bathrooms should, above all, be relaxing and aesthetically pleasing. However, before you can enjoy arranging your exquisite jars of essential oils or work out the perfect place to hang your flower prints, you need to establish practical places for everyday items.

- Ceilings can be fitted with hanging racks on a pulley. Use them to store towels, loofahs and brushes.

- Use cutlery trays and small baskets to keep cosmetics and toiletries in order. Alternatively, fit the inside of a cupboard door with a wire spice rack from a kitchen manufacturer.

- As well as looking attractive, a traditional pegboard hung with large baskets makes a good home for towels and facecloths.

- A small laundry basket, either freestanding or the kind that swings open from behind a cupboard door, provides a quick and easy place to stash bathtime toys.

- Make the most of tall ceilings by adding a high shelf which runs all the way around the room. Exploit its decorative potential as a home for pretty containers, vases and pictures; use it practically to store extra towels and a medicine box.

OTHER PLACES

If you have exploited every inch of available space in the main areas of your home and you still find wardrobes bursting with clothes and drawers crammed with a jumble of possessions, don't despair.

It is highly likely that you have more storage space at your disposal than you think. Investigate all the 'forgotten spaces' such as attics, cellars, garages, hallways and landings, and assess how they might best be used to ease your storage problems.

MAXIMUM EXPLOITATION

Modern-day living often requires that we make the most of every last corner of our homes; decorating and furnishing the main rooms is only the beginning. As households grow and change, they often have to absorb new people, new work patterns and new hobbies. Your storage solutions should be flexible enough to accommodate these changes and to adapt along with you.

The arrival of children, or their attaining different levels of maturity, can produce a whole new set of storage challenges. Not only do you have to furnish their rooms, but their presence often puts more pressure on the rest of the house; previously unexplored nooks and crannies are suddenly filled with shelves, and alcoves are fitted with cupboards or lined with drawers.

And even without children, the way in which we live now makes a whole new set of demands on our space. Many homes now contain home offices and even gyms – something that was relatively rare only a few years ago.

But in most homes, the space can be found to cater for our new requirements. Halls, cellars, attics, garages and other frequently unexplored areas can all be made to work harder than they do.

Working at home

The number of people now working from home has risen dramatically in recent years. And even for those who do go out to work, it is a rare household that can do without a quiet corner dedicated specifically to writing letters or doing family accounts. This need not mean a separate office, however. With some imagination and careful planning, it is possible to combine a successful home office with the rest of your living area, even when space is limited.

Bedrooms, dining rooms and living rooms can be divided with open-backed storage units, either in the form of basic shelves or a series of cubes. Some manufacturers sell these with coordinating drawer and cupboard units, to conceal less attractive items. Alternatively, you could cover part of the system with a simple blind. You can also divide any suitable corner or alcove from the rest of the room with curtains or a screen.

To prevent your office space from overwhelming the rest of the room, try to keep the furniture simple. Dining tables make generous desks; smaller drop-leaf tables stand neatly against the wall, to be brought out when needed; table tops that are hinged against the wall with supporting struts are also useful. Folding chairs can be hung on the wall when not in use.

In some schemes, antique or second-hand pieces are more appropriate. Look out for old shop display cabinets, wooden filing cabinets and architects' plan chests. For some items, however, modern solutions are best. Printers, small photocopiers and fax machines are more secure on sturdy metal trolleys. These are easily wheeled out of sight when not in use and you can even conceal them completely beneath a skirted table.

Stationery and office supplies can be stored in all kinds of containers, depending on your scheme. Small boxes with numerous drawers or compartments are very useful, while hatboxes, baskets and terracotta plant pots take the hard edge off the display.

THE PLEASURE PRINCIPLE

Good storage should be functional, but it should also harmonize with the surroundings and reflect your own personality and lifestyle.

The hallway of this busy family house (left) is lively and inviting. A cupboard provides space for coats and shoes while favourite books and toys line deep bookshelves. The side of the bookcase has been given a coat of blackboard paint to transform it into a convenient noticeboard that no member of the family can miss.

This illustrator's bookcase (page 66) houses all the tools of the trade but at the same time it doesn't stint on style – with a bright collection of jars, bottles, pots and pieces of artwork lending visual interest.

Terracotta plant pots painted in attractive colours help to keep pencils, paints and brushes organized in this artist's studio (page 67).

BEDTIME STORIES

The bed is the main piece of furniture in most children's rooms, so it is worth considering all of the possibilities open to you.

- A small platform with a mattress on top and fitted with drawers, cupboard doors or fabric curtains below provides generous storage for clothes, books and toys.

- A modular platform bed, suitable for children from around seven years of age, allows the bed to be moved higher as children get older. Eventually, you could even install a desk or sofa beneath.

- Concealing a pull-out bed under a child's single bed will provide valuable sleeping accommodation for any young guests.

- You might also want to look out for 'bed in a bag' products – a roll-out foam mattress and a sleeping bag with an integral pillow. They take up very little space and you will be able to use them time and time again.

- When two or more children have to share the same bedroom, position a wardrobe, a set of drawers or bookshelves between the beds. This will provide valuable storage space and add a sense of privacy.

70 ■

KIDS' STUFF

Children's rooms set very specific demands. The storage you choose needs to be secure and safe and it should also grow with the child. Modular pieces provide the necessary flexibility in this colourful and functional bedroom (left). Not only can they be used to create a sleeping platform with desk space beneath, but smaller spaces can be made for tall books, toys and games.

This pretty room appeals to the child's sense of fantasy (right). Striking drapes in an unusual colour combination shield the bed from the rest of the room while a coordinating trunk stores bedding and doubles up as a bedside table. Beneath the bed, wooden crates on castors have been painted to complement the rest of the scheme and form handy pull-out drawers for toys and clothes.

Tips for tidy children

As your children grow and change, so do their storage needs. It is wise to consider not just what they need today, but how it could be adapted when they are older. For example, a sturdy bookcase can store clothes, toiletries and toys for a baby, then books and games and, later still, could provide a home for a teenager's stereo equipment.

Choose bookcases with adjustable shelves for maximum flexibility and pay close attention to their stability. If your floors are uneven or if the shelves are heavily loaded, it is a good idea to fix them to the wall or floor with screws and/or brackets. Wall-mounted shelves on metal track-and-bracket fixings are also worth considering, as they allow you to tailor shelves to fit every available nook and cranny.

Babies and small children require little wardrobe space so if you are working to a budget, steer clear of charming but expensive miniature children's furniture. By the time your child needs a wardrobe, you can adapt an adult one, perhaps by lowering the hanging rail and filling the space above with shelves for sweaters and T-shirts. In the meantime, pegboards or rails attached to the wall will

The space under the stairs is often neglected and even when it is used, it can be difficult to get at. This is a waste, as often it is one of the few areas we have that is spacious enough to store bulky things such as vacuum cleaners, brooms and ironing boards. Adapt your cupboard with the help of some of the hooks, holders and door shelving units available from kitchen and storage specialists. Here, the door has been cut so that it fits perfectly with the shape of the steps (above).

probably provide sufficient hanging space. Coat hooks on the backs of doors and hanging organizer panels with lots of pockets will encourage even small children to put their own things away.

A small chest of drawers is a good investment in a child's room. In the early stages, the top can be used as a changing surface and later it makes a good play or display table. Office trolleys with sliding drawers or single-drawer filing units also provide storage space for toys or clothes.

Toy boxes and chests will get lots of use so they need to be strong and capacious if your child is not to outgrow them quickly. Plastic stacking boxes in bright colours are also a popular and inexpensive way of storing toys. You could even try colour coding them to encourage your child to tidy up: blue for bricks, red for soft toys; yellow for dressing-up clothes, and so on.

Smaller toys can be kept in cutlery trays, fold-out tool chests and plastic or tin toy buckets. A child with an extensive collection of soft toys may enjoy clipping them to a length of bright cord or ribbon with clothes pegs and then suspending them from the wall, door or ceiling. To save your sanity, it is a good idea to provide some extra children's storage in other rooms of the house such as a bookshelf dedicated to their things in the kitchen, a blanket box in the sitting room or a small laundry basket in the bathroom.

Neglected spaces

Hallways and landings often have a great deal of untapped storage potential. Think creatively about these spaces and you could transform the way you use your home. Does a half landing lend itself to a window seat with storage

Hallways often contain an abundance of generous, underused space. They are also the most public areas in our homes, the ones that all of our visitors see, so it's worth giving some thought to the kind of impression you are making.

In this calm and stylish hallway (centre left), the space under the stairs has been filled with roomy pull-out shelves. The honeyed tones of the wood blend perfectly with the soft, earthy colour scheme and frosted glass panels add an airy feel. Cut-out handles make it easy to open the drawers and also allow the air to circulate.

In this striking hall (left), stone steps provide the starting point for a set of dark wood shelves formally arranged with books, magazines and African pottery. As well as providing generous storage space, this combination of muted colours and rich textures makes a strong visual impression.

space inside? Could you install a writing desk in the hall? Would it be possible to convert the space under the stairs into a sewing corner or laundry area?

Before you embark on any grandiose plans for the hall, you need to consider this space in exactly the same way as you would any other room and examine what you require from it. This is one place that every member of the household passes through several times a day so, to make life simpler, consider where the best place to store outdoor clothes and frequently used sports equipment would be.

Some people choose to line their halls with shelves and cupboards, which can transform a hitherto bland space into a cosy and welcoming entrance. This kind of built-in storage is useful if you have bulky items, such as suitcases or winter bedding, which have failed to find a home elsewhere in the house. Filling the space under the stairs with shelves, storage boxes and strong hooks will also help to keep the hall free of unsightly clutter.

Even if you are blessed with ample storage in the other rooms and don't need to use your hall, it is worth considering the visual impact of housing some of your favourite possessions here. A beautifully arranged collection of ceramics, walls lined with books or a corner full of framed family pictures all say something about who you are and set the tone for the house.

When you are deciding on the decor for the staircase and landing remember that, along with the hallway, this

HAPPY LANDINGS

Mezzanine levels are an inspired solution for tall rooms. A platform built high in the eaves of this loft makes enough space for two attractive fabric wardrobes reminiscent of old-fashioned bathing huts.

Large baskets store extra cushions and bedding and a sturdy step ladder makes for easy access.

If you have a high enough room to create a mezzanine level, consider using it to house a home office or spare bedroom. Lined with books and with the addition of a comfortable chair, a mezzanine also makes a calm, meditative reading corner.

Many of us are filled with good intentions to recycle our rubbish and, at last, ecologically minded manufacturers have developed products to make it easier to do (left).

Newspaper and bottle holders are quite commonplace now, as are special bins with separate compartments for paper, tin and glass products.

Outdoor space can sometimes be a resting home for the unloved and unused, and it can quickly deteriorate into chaos.

This narrow outbuilding is exemplary in its order. Inexpensive modular units hold extensive supplies of comestibles and drawers hold small tools and household accessories. Hooks on the wall and ceiling keep sports equipment secure while crates allow beer and wine to be stored on their side. A cupboard for out-of-season clothes has been created by covering a modular cube with a roller blind.

As with storage in the rest of the house, the more time you give to outdoor storage in the planning stage, the more likely you are to maintain it in its pristine state. Your best ally in keeping the space tidy is a good stable stepladder – you may even want to think about installing library-style steps that run along a wall of shelves.

space constitutes the main artery of your home. It should be decorated harmoniously to create a sense of the space flowing easily from room to room. Keep colours, textures and details, such as the mouldings on cupboards and shelves, consistent.

If your house has an attic, could a few simple alterations make it work harder for you? A strong, pull-down ladder and basic lighting will help to render this space usable. Fill it with inexpensive shelving stacked with the things you

scarcely use but can't throw out and you will immediately increase your sense of order downstairs.

Similarly, any dry cellar or garage space can be turned to advantage. Small cellars can be lined with racks to store wine and water bottles and larger cellars can take a lot of the overflow from the kitchen. Big chest freezers are often better kept out of the kitchen, where they take up a great deal of space. Flexible modular shelving gives you an opportunity to transform a cellar or garage into an old-

BEHIND CLOSED DOORS

If you have a large bathroom you could consider partitioning part of it off to create a laundry area. There are three natural advantages to this: you can keep plumbing costs to a minimum because all the necessary pipes are already installed; tiled and damp-proof surfaces mean easy maintenance; and dirty laundry can easily be collected and transferred to the washing machine.

To ensure that it does not intrude on the bathroom space, conceal your laundry equipment behind a screen wall. Concertina doors make the least intrusion on the floor space.

Alternatively, if you are a fitness fanatic, you may want to convert an unused cellar or garage into a fully fledged gym.

Tools, workbenches and all of the attendant craft and home-maintenance essentials can be kept in these spaces, away from the main household. A small chest of drawers should be sufficient to meet most requirements, particularly when combined with wall hanging space. You might want to try fixing a piece of pegboard to the wall along with hooks from which to hang all of the tools. Once you have arranged them to your satisfaction, take a thick felt-tip pen and draw a silhouette around each one. This way, each piece is returned to the same spot so that you don't waste time hunting for things – and you can see at a glance if something is missing.

fashioned, practical 'larder' away from the heat and humidity of the kitchen. For the thrifty, canned food, vinegar, bottles of oil, cleaning products, lavatory paper, bags of rice and flour, some root vegetables and fruit can be bought more cheaply in bulk and then stored here. This kind of buying, however, is usually best suited to households where the turnover of food is high.

Laundry equipment can also be kept in the cellar, where the noise of the motors won't irritate you. If you are short on space, look out for combination washer-driers, tumble driers that stack on top of washing machines and compact appliances. These can be up to a third smaller than standard machines, but work just as well and are ideal for couples or people who live alone.

Sports equipment can be conveniently stored in a cellar or secure garage. Special hanging racks for skis, bicycles and rackets can be fixed securely to the wall or ceiling.

WALL TO WALL

Laundry equipment takes up a lot of space and can often make a room look messy. If you can't house it in a separate room, conceal it behind a wall of fitted cupboards (left).

In this office-cum-utility room, vented doors ingeniously conceal a washing machine and drier. A solid door hides a space-saving, fold-out ironing board and drawers provide plenty of space for household linen and cleaning equipment.

INDEX

PUBLISHER'S ACKNOWLEDGMENTS

We would like to thank the following photographers and organizations for their permission to reproduce the photographs in this book:

1 Sue Pitman, Steve Dalton (The Holding Company, 243-245, King's Rd, London SW3 5EL; 0171–352 1600.); 2 Peter Cook (Architect: Jonathan Woolf)/Hilary Coe; 3 Sue Pitman, Steve Dalton (The Holding Company); 4-5 Peter Woloszynski/The Interior Archive; 6-7 Ron Sutherland; 7 Neil Lorimer/Elizabeth Whiting & Associates; 8 Alberto Piovano (Architect: Francisco Rius)/Arcaid; 9 Alberto Piovano (Architect: Francisco Rius)/Arcaid; 10-11 Otto Polman, Hans Zeegers/Ariadne, Holland; 12-13 Michael Freeman (Owner: Miranda Rothschild); 14 above Jerome Darblay; 14 below Lars Hallen; 15 Bernard Touillon/ Coté Sud/ Elizabeth Whiting & Associates; 16-17 Hotze Eisma/V.T. Wonen, Holland; 17 Simon Brown/Elle Decoration; 18-19 Damien Gillie/Elle Decoration; 20 Peter Cook (Architect: Jonathan Woolf)/Hilary Coe; 21 below Rodney Hyett/ Elizabeth Whiting & Associates; 21 above Paul Ryan/International Interiors; 23 Schöner Wohnen/Camera Press; 24 Marie Pierre Morel (Stylists: Le Signe, Puech)/Marie Claire Maison; 25 Tim Street-Porter (Designer: Tom Callaway); 26 Peter Baistow; 27 Simon Wheeler/ Elle Decoration; 28 Sue Pitman, Steve Dalton (The Holding Company); 29 right Sue Pitman, Steve Dalton (The Holding Company); 29 left Pierre Hussenot (Stylists: Veronique Roy, Anne-Marie Comte)/Marie Claire Maison; 30 Florian Bolk, Maria Quemada/La Casa de Marie Claire/Gruner & Jahr AG & Co.; 31 Jean Caillaut (Stylist: Catherine Ardouin)/Marie Claire Maison; 32 Alberto Piovano (Architect: Marco Romanelli)/Arcaid; 32-33 Bill Batten (Stylist: Jane Cumberbatch)/Elle Decoration; 34 Alberto Piovano (Architect: Pierre d'Avoine)/Arcaid; 35 Guillaume de Laubier/Scoop; 36-37 Simon Wheeler/Scoop; 37 below David Phelps; 37 above Jonathan Pilkington; 38 right Schöner Wohnen/ Camera Press; 38 left Yves Duronsoy/S.I.P./Elizabeth Whiting & Associates; 39 above Simon McBride; 40 right Conran Octopus/Simon Brown; 40 left Alexandre Bailhache (Stylist: Marie Guibert)/Marie Claire Maison; 41 John van Groenendaal/Eigenhuis & Interieur, Holland; 42-43 Simon Brown/The Interior Archive; 43 Paul Grootes/Ariadne, Holland; 44 Christophe Dugied (Stylist: Julie Borgeaud)/Marie Claire Maison; 45 Fritz von der Schulenburg (Robert Nadler)/The Interior Archive; 46 David Phelps; 47 right Ron Arad & Associates Ltd; 47 left Nicolas Tosi (Stylists: Borgeaud, Comte)/Marie Claire Maison; 48 below Hans Zeegers/Ariadne, Holland; 48 above Otto Polman, Hans Zeegers/ Ariadne, Holland; 49 Tim Street-Porter (Architect: Scott Johnson); 50 Conran Octopus/Simon Brown; 51 Conran Octopus/Simon Brown; 52 Tim Street-Porter (Architect: Scott Johnson); 53 left Guillaume de Laubier/Elle Decoration/ Scoop; 54-55 Gille de Chabaneix (Stylist: Catherine Ardouin)/Marie Claire Maison; 54 right Guillaume de Laubier/Elle Decoration/Scoop; 55 Abitare; 56 Richard Bryant (Architects: GEA; Interior Designer: Madame Pommereau)/Arcaid; 57 Richard Bryant (Architects: GEA; Interior Designer: Madame Pommereau)/Arcaid; 58 Jacques Dirand (Appartment: Christian Lacroix)/Maison Française/Stylograph; 60 Bernard Touillon/ S.I.P./Elizabeth Whiting & Associates; 61 left Simon Wheeler/Elle Decoration; 61 left Marie Pierre Morel (Stylist: Julie Borgeaud)/Marie Claire Maison; 62 Henry Wilson (Designer: Ray Oxley); 63 Paul Ryan/International Interiors; 64 left Peter Cook (Architect: Tugman Partnership)/Hilary Coe; 64 right Eduardo Munoz/La Casa de Marie Claire/Gruner & Jahr AG & Co.; 65 Christopher Drake/Robert Harding Syndication; 66-67 Albert Roosenburg/V.T. Wonen, Holland; 67 Eric Morin/Coté Sud/Elizabeth Whiting & Associates; 68-69 Brigitte/ Camera Press; 70 Brigitte/ Camera Press; 71 Hotze Eisma/Ariadne Holland; 72 left Hotze Eisma/Eigenhuis & Interieur, Holland; 72-73 Andreas von Einsiedel/ Elizabeth Whiting & Associates; 73 Nicolas Tosi (Stylists: Julie Borgeaud, Ann-Marie Comte)/Marie Claire Maison; 74 Rob van Uchelen/Ariadne, Holland; 75 Zuhause/ Camera Press; 76 Russell Brooks/Australian House & Gardens Bathrooms; 77 right Simon Kenny (Architect: Caroline Pidcock)/ Vogue Living (Australia); 77 left Simon Kenny (Architect: Caroline Pidcock)/Vogue Living (Australia).

AUTHOR'S ACKNOWLEDGMENTS

I have many people to thank for help with this book. At Homes & Ideas, my friend Virginia Hiller is an inspiring colleague from whom I learn much every day.

At Conran Octopus, the highly talented team made this book a real pleasure to work on. With their unstinting enthusiasm and hard work, Claire Taylor and Alison Barclay, made the whole thing look wonderful. I am truly indebted to Jane Chapman; her patience and attention to detail in the editing of the project was a constant inspiration. I would also like to thank Denny Hemming and John Wallace for their much valued encouragement. Without Helen Lewis' friendship and wicked sense of humour, my life would be a lot less colourful. Finally, a big thank you to my agent, Juliet Burton, and to Dawna Walter of The Holding Company, the tidiest woman in London, who inspired me to neater heights.